RICH
THINKING

The Fundamentals Of Abundance

By: Dr. Eddie Powell

Eddie@EddiePowell.com

Photos By: Shirley Evans

What is Rich Thinking?

Rich Thinking encompasses all that we are, all that we do, all that we are stewards of, and all that we temporary control of throughout our journey called "Life".

Rich Thinking seeks to provide some deeper understanding based on Biblical passages, translations, and meanings to bring into focus and perspective the physical riches and wealth intended for each and every Believer.

Throughout the ages, many have come to envy, despise, and want to do harm to those that have riches, especially money. Never stopping to realize that without God allowing it or blessing them with the riches, they would never have them.

Further, each and every Believer is meant to be rich, is meant to be blessed with land, real estate, business, cattle on every hill, and much, much more. I invite you to read Deuteronomy 28 in the Bible for the listing of the blessings you are entitled to as a Christian follower of

Jesus and the curses should you revoke Jesus from your life. Please remember, this is Bible, not something that I made up.

Welcome to Rich Thinking!

Rich Thinking: It is your choice.

Inside each of us is a brain that has been programmed over the years and through our family and many associations to think certain things. We have been taught to match color combinations in our attire. We have been taught the rules of the road for driving our automobiles. We have even been taught right from wrong.

Within this collective learning, we have learned or developed an awareness of rich and poor or wealth and poverty. If your parents were quick to remind you that you cannot have everything you ask for because "we're not made of money" or "money doesn't grow on trees" then quite probably you have developed a great awareness of money or rather, the lack of it.

With many people, those ideas have become foundational and are never revisited to determine if they are serving us well. In fact, they are adopted as truth and passed along to future generations without question.

Well, I would suggest to you that today is the day to review those ideas and perhaps replace them with some ideas that could better serve you, that is, if you are tired of the poverty, the struggle, the stress of wondering where the next rent payment or grocery money is going to come from. I admit that some people seem to get hold of an idea, any idea, and want to own it to the death, no matter what or who shows them evidence otherwise. I say to them, I admire your determination and respect your right to your beliefs. To you, I offer that you may want to lay this book aside right now and not bother yourself with it at all, seeing as you are already "set in your ways" as my grandmother used to say.

For the rest of us – and that includes you, since you are obviously still reading – I offer up some Biblical-based evidence that God wants you rich! I present this in a conversational manner rather than a scholarly read fully of cites and quotes. I invite you to get out your Bible and do some reading and investigating of your own or perhaps you want to obtain an electronic version for your computer and search terms to read the surrounding text to which I am referring. Either way, time well spent, I would suggest.

Over the years, I think some of the preachers have gone the way of today's media, as they discovered that drama sells. They grabbed on to the fire-and-brimstone side of the Bible, only to forsake the love, peace, and grace facets of

God. In my way of thinking, we are God's children, welcome into the Kingdom, heirs to the throne just as Jesus is, and if all the streets in heaven are made of gold, then, riches are not a problem to My Daddy, Father, God.

Thinking that God wants me rich just makes sense to me. He knows that to do the works, tools must be used and one of those tools is money. Ah, some say that is why there are people or angels and such. I say, if you were a carpenter and the only tool you had in your toolbox was one hammer, then there is a lot of things that you may attempt to build that will not come out looking like they were supposed to. Same here, money, people, angels, words, prayers, and much more are all tools that we can use to help do our part to accomplish His will and purpose… "Your will be done on earth as it is in heaven."

So, let's just focus on a thought at the top of the page.

Then, take a little journey through the many stories and

pages of the Bible and recall what it says about that aspect

of :   Rich Thinking – The Fundamentals of Abundance.

Money comes to me in ways that I could never have imagined.

Don't limit God with your expectations. Allow Him to surprise you. He will amaze you with His wonder. I have found over the years that one of the delights of His heart is to do or arrange the unexpected.

Certainly, God is a God of miracles but many times He saves miracles as a last resort. I believe His first choice is to use men, women, and children to do as He instructs them. Sometimes they do not hear Him. Other times they have a hard time with whatever He is instructing them to do, to the point that they choose not to do this thing. The disappointing part of them not doing as they are instructed is that they miss the blessing He had in store for them, if they had only followed His instruction through the Holy Spirit.

Sometimes it seems to take so long for your prayer to be answered. Many times this is due to the doubt one person or many people may have to complete this leading. Other times His eyes search to and fro to find someone that is "available" yet comes up with no one. This could delay things until someone that offers themselves as "available" comes along, seeking to do His will, as instructed.

No one available may even move God to choose another way, many times we call them miracles due to how they are positioned relative to the normal physical day-to-day methods of operation. For instance, in the Bible, Jesus had to pay taxes. God simply brought a fish to the surface that spit out the coins that He needed. Other stories tell of talking donkey's, birds of the air that brought manna to the Prophet, rocks that Moses hit with his stick and then produced water, even the Red Sea being parted so the Jews could escape Egypt was another example of a miracle.

Is it beyond God to move people on your behalf? Is it beyond God to perform a miracle for you to receive your needs met? Absolutely not! God is no respecter of persons. That means, He bows to no one, none is higher, no person with or without a title intimidates Him. In addition, He chooses who He blesses, who He will do miracles for, and what actions He will take toward whom. He searches hearts to know the meaning and intent of the person. This is something that is impossible to hide from God.

God knows then if you are trapped in a cycle of serving money more than serving Him. He knows if your heart is full of gratitude and thanks. He knows the intended use and the works you have done previously and even whether you have asked forgiveness for any past thoughts or actions that do not line up with God's way of doing and being right.

God knows all. Truth is, you can run but you can never hide from God. This means, you cannot hide from God and you cannot hide from God's blessings. I recall the story of Jacob, who was sold into slavery by his brothers. Even though he was cast into prison, God's blessings tracked him down and blessed him to the overwhelming extent that the Pharaoh of Egypt promoted Jacob to be second in command of all Egypt. During the drought, Jacob was in charge of food and feeding all of Egypt.

Point is, no matter the situation you are facing right now, God can get His blessing to you, He can raise you up, and He can lead you out. Your duty is to remain available, listen and follow His word, take action when He tells you to take action, and remain forever in a state of gratitude and praise for God. God must remain first in your life, not the money, not the other blessings. Only God can cause you to prosper. Lose sight of that and He can allow it all to be taken away just as quickly.

I welcome and expect money.

The Bible tells us in Deuteronomy 28 the many ways God blesses us: coming in and going out, in the city and in the field, in everything that we set our hands to, and much more. This is certainly worth reading. God has blessed us, each and every one of His children, His believers.

God wants us to enjoy life more abundantly. This means He wants us rich, wealthy, prosperous, rich in cattle, rich in real estate, abundant and prosperous in all that we do to the point that we shall lend and never borrow for the borrower is the servant of the lender.

The Bible tells us that the love of money is the root of all evil. Notice, it is the love of money, not the money itself.

Money in and of itself is neutral. It is the intent in the heart of the person(s) that uses money to perform blessings or evil actions, the money has nothing to do with it.

God wants us as the head and not the tail. God wants us to be conquers not victims. Notice that poverty, death, sickness, and destruction are all under the curse of the law. Jesus broke that curse by descending unto hell, getting the keys, and ascending to heaven to sit on the right hand of God forevermore. The devil has no power, other than what we are deceived into allowing him via our lack of understanding or confusion.

The devil trying to tell us that rich people must be doing something evil to gain all of that money or rich people are always trying to beat the little guy out of all his money, too. This is all distortion and lies. Admittedly, there are crooks in every line of work but many rich people actually do many wonderful things with their fortunes, primary example being Andrew Carnegie, a steel manufacturer that endowed many noble causes including libraries all across the United States and other educational entities including Carnegie Hall for the benefit of the people. Colleges and universities have benefited from rich people and their endowments, so have foundations, nonprofit agencies, medicine, research, and much more.

Truth is, God wants more people to realize that they are blessed. They no longer have to live in poverty, sickness, or under the curse. Jesus broke the yokes and set the captives free so that they might live life more abundantly. Translated, this means rich in love, rich in peace, rich in prosperity, rich in abundance including family, rich in gentleness, kindness, mercy, and patience. Rich in wealth, businesses, gold, silver, gems, real estate, and so much more.

Once we get this down on the inside of us, in our heart, planted as a seed, watered, cared for, fed, brought out into the sunshine, and allowed to grow, it will become huge and key for our rich and abundant future.

Jesus wants you blessed. All you have to do is believe in Him, accept all He has said of you, all He has set aside for you, and live the abundant life that He has laid out for you. Believe, receive, and you shall have what you ask for in Jesus name.

Take a moment here to reflect on your blessings with gratitude and thanks. (Make notes, if you'd like.)

I am a financially free person.

God set forth in covenant with Abraham in Deuteronomy

28 and elsewhere that every believer is blessed. You obtain

this blessing as soon as you are born again into the

Kingdom of God, simply by believing and claiming Jesus

as your Lord and Savior. This simple prayer act

transforms you into the Kingdom and saves your soul for

eternity. As a Kingdom member, you are entitled to all the rights and privileges including the blessing, riches, and glory.

Jesus is our living example here on earth. He traveled healing and performing many miracles. Yet one thing that many people overlook is that Jesus had disciples that journeyed with Him and learned from Him before setting out on their own. During this time, Judas was always nearby. Judas was the treasurer for Jesus. Frankly, why would Jesus need a treasurer, if there were no money coming into and being distributed out of His ministry? Understand, Jesus was rich. Streets made of gold in heaven, pearly gates, God loves beauty and riches to further do His will and purpose.

God wants each and every one of His followers rich so that the funds can be used to do the works of His ministry, bless others, and be an illustration to others outside the Kingdom as to the riches of God. Otherwise, who would want to join the Kingdom to give up, be beat up, and downtrodden. Heck, being a victim is easy. It takes faith and courage to boldly take the Kingdom by storm and be the living example of Jesus… and all of that takes money (you don't think God knows that?)

I attract money.

Wisdom, knowledge, and understanding are the principle things. But, above all, get wisdom for she shall keep thee, and understanding. Think about this, wisdom, knowledge, and understanding will help you get riches and wealth. With wisdom, knowledge, and understanding you can recognize opportunity, exercise your talents to earn even more riches (read the parable of the talents), and be successful in business so that others come to you to do business and learn.

Think of it, to be a blacksmith, you studied or apprenticed with the blacksmith. To be a carpenter, you studied with the carpenter. To be an Apostle, you studied with the Master, Jesus. In all these cases, you received with gratitude, you welcomed the blessings bestowed upon you, and eventually, you not only lived the life but passed your knowledge, wisdom, and understanding on to the next person that was deemed worthy to study with you.

Studying Jesus, you would have learned His love, His ways, His miracles (even Peter walked on the water until he lost focus on Jesus), and even His abundance and riches. The more you seek to become like Jesus, the more you must recognize and accept the money and riches to benefit others. In fact, not accepting and recognizing the riches and abundance so that you can help more and more people would be a sin because you are depriving others of their needs being met. God will then have to move through some other person or perform a miracle to accomplish the goal.

Do not deny God, instead, stand with your arms outstretched and tell Him you are available. Then, allow Him to do His work through you.

I can feel my wealth grow on a daily basis.

God's will and purpose for your life is what you need to dial into. In every case, God is going to raise you up while providing you with the tools, talents, skills, and people needed for each event or activity He places you in.

I liken this to a motorboat crossing the water. God does not get you out into the middle of the lake then shut down the motor. No, God has the power to get you from one shore to the other, in the right time, in the right place, with the right people, and in time for the right event to allow for your purpose as you have agreed with His will and purpose.

You don't need to second guess, argue, wonder, or question God's motives. He is a wonderful God fully able to do all He has set in motion and all He has ordained. You can remove all fear and doubt from your heart and from your conversations right now.. it is no longer needed nor useful. Only faith in God is valid and valuable. In fact, faith in the now… or "Now faith" is the substance of things hoped for and the evidence of things not seen. Faith, hope, evidence of things not seen – truth is, you wouldn't need any faith if you could already see the thing. So, our faith is the currency that brings all that we do not yet see into the physical realm where we can see it, touch it, smell it, and understand its reality.

Look around you, these are the things that you had faith currency for in the past. They have materialized around you through some God and faith means. They have created the picture you are standing in.

If you consider the picture you are standing in and say to yourself that something is missing, perhaps, a new car, a new couch, or even a new house. Utilizing your faith currency, trusting in God, keeping up with the Rich Thinking, and soon enough your picture will have changed to include whatever it is that you are now focusing on. Now Faith is the substance, evidence, the faith currency needed to remain strong and true for the new items to appear in your new picture. This is exactly how you make your "New Future" appear.

Faith without works is dead.

Now Faith takes advantage of opportunity. It stays focused on the desired outcomes. Truth is, operating Now Faith has a plan, with clarity focused on what the hopes are, and the action(s) taken to bring forth the things not yet seen.

Being the blessing for others keeps you focused on blessings. Soon blessings will begin to come to you just as you are continuing to take blessings to them. In fact, the more you bless others, the more you bless yourself. The Bible speaks of 10-fold, 30-fold, 60-fold, 100-fold, and multi-fold blessings along with generational blessings. Do you think that previous generations in your family line may not have used all of their generational blessings? Then, ask the Lord to move forward their generational blessings to you, that you may have extra portions. Watch your world begin to change even more rapidly for the positive.

Be the blessing. Give to multiply. Release and forgive all others. For as you forgive others, the Lord can forgive you. Walk in love. Most importantly, Love the Lord God with all your heart, all your mind, and all your body. Seek to do His ways and His will, for His ways are higher than your ways, His will is above your will. His knowledge surpasses all understanding.

Expect, receive, and fully walk in your blessings, always thanking and praising God. For this is Rich Thinking which makes for an abundant and prosperous life.

Remember, only the body is cast aside. Life is forever…

Live it richly!

Eddie Powell   +   Shirley Evans

Eddie Powell is available for speaking, teaching, and

consulting.

Contact: Eddie Powell

Eddie@EddiePowell.com

For Availability

GOD WANTS YOU RICH…

…Prosperous

…Abundant

…Wealthy

…Blessed In The City

…Blessed In The Field

…Blessed Coming In

…Blessed Going Out

…Blessed In Real Estate

…Blessed In Business

…Blessed In Everything You Lay Your Hand To

I Will Say It Again So It Get's Down On The Inside Of You…

GOD WANTS YOU RICH…

Repeat This Over and Over

To Get It Planted

Deep Down in Your Soul

Say It Out Loud…

GOD WANTS ME RICH…

Again, Say It Out Loud…

GOD WANTS ME RICH…

…Me

…My Family

…My Children

…My Children's Children

…and All The Generations To Come!

RICH THINKING

The Fundamentals Of Abundance

By: Dr. Eddie Powell

Refresh With Stories From
The Bible That Renew Your
Hope, Faith, & Trust In God

Rejoice… For Amazing
Changes Can Be Yours

KNOWLEDGE, WISDOM, & UNDERSTANDING RICH THINKING INSIGHTS

Build Your Faith – Develop
Your Gratitude
Appreciation

Exclusive Audio Presentations
Including Targeted Sessions For:
Women, Youth, Seniors, Entrepreneurs/Businesses,
Non-Profits/Churches, and More

RICH THINKING

The Fundamentals Of Abundance

By: Dr. Eddie Powell

Jesus Lead By Example

Jesus Was Rich…

Otherwise, Why Would Jesus' Ministry Have

Need Of A Treasurer?

(Yes, Judas Was Jesus' Treasurer… Known

For Distributing Money To The Poor)

Jesus Himself said,

"I Am Come That They Might Have Life,

And That They Might Have It More

Abundantly." (John 10:10)

TAKE

ACTION NOW

Reinforce Your Learning With Daily

Affirmations

<u>Remember: **YOU HAVE VALUE!**</u>

RICH THINKING

The Fundamentals Of
Abundance

By: Dr. Eddie Powell

Dr. Eddie Powell, Doctor of Divinity, is included in

www.LinkedIn.com/in/EddiePowell and has been honored with a

U.S. Presidential Commission,

U.S. Congressional Order of Merit, and as the U.S. Small Business

Administration 2007 Journalist of the Year – Region V (Entire

Midwest + Highest Award Possible).

Dr. Powell encourages you to take action and move your thinking

into a new realm of possibilities with Rich Thinking-The

Fundamentals of Abundance

Look For Many Other Books From

Dr. Eddie Powell

On Amazon + Kindle Available Worldwide

Enjoy!

Remember,

God Wants You

Rich!